Dedicated To

Albert V. Schoonmaker
and Norma Schwartz

Contents

So you want to play Jazz...

Great! Playing Jazz styles on the piano is one of the most creative endeavors a person could embark upon. In the process of playing "Piano Jazz" you will become a master theorist, composer, and arranger. Each of these components is an essential puzzle piece used in creating the mosaic we call Jazz.

The foundation and cornerstone of Jazz Piano is theory, or, putting it In a better way, Jazz harmony. The word "Jazz" is derived from an African Language and means "surprise". So the master Jazz player knows all the rules of chord progressions (movements of chords), and therefore can freely twist and turn them spontaneously so that he is even surprising himself. Practice becomes an adventure in experimentation and is never the dull tedium of repeating the same phrases ad infinitum.

The first step is learning the basic seventh chords. The first chord we learn is the Major seventh chord. It is derived directly from the Major scale:

We play Jazz on the piano from "lead sheets" and "fake-books" which give us the melody and the chord symbols. The way we play the song and "voice" the chords is up to us (much more about that later).

So, we have to able to tell what the chord is immediately from the symbol.

The chord symbol for the Major seventh can appear in several ways:

CMaj.7, CM7, or in recent times CΔ7

It is important that you know all three symbols. It is also essential that you know exactly what the chord "contains". The Major seventh has a root, a Major third, a fifth, and a Major seventh.

A close cousin of the Major seventh chord is the Major sixth chord. The symbol usually looks like this:

C6

It contains a root, a Major third, a fifth, and a Major sixth. It is also derived from the Major scale:

The Major sixth has a very consonant sound and so is very often used for ending a phrase or a song. It is also used as a "substitute" for a Major 7th chord, so that there is another sound to pair with the Major 7th.

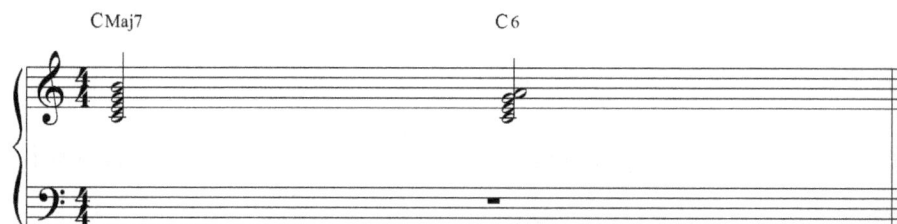

The next chord you will learn is the dominant 7th which is the most powerful and tension-filled chord, hence the name: DOMINANT. This is due to the fact that the chord contains a Major 3rd which is pitted against a minor 7th. This creates the "tri-tone" interval, also known as the "devil's interval". It is considered the most dissonant of all intervals! If you ever watch foreign films, you will notice the sound of the ambulance sirens: a repetitive tri-tone! In composition classes, students are told to avoid a tri-tone in writing melodies. Leonard Bernstein, however, ignored this caveat when writing "Maria", the beautiful ballad from "West Side Story".

Here is an example of several dominant seventh chords:

The dominant seventh chord contains a root, a Major third, a fifth, and a minor seventh. The symbol for a dominant seventh is mysterious in that It has no sign to tell us that it is dominant. It simply appears as a letter and an Arabic numeral:

C7, G7, D7, A7

Chord number three is the minor seventh. It is a very pretty sounding chord, and is used all the time as a precedent sound to the dominant seventh chord, creating the most common of all progressions: the II-V-I.

The minor seventh chord contains a root, a minor third, a fifth, and a minor seventh:

The next chord is enigmatic as it really has two names. It can be called a minor seventh with a flatted fifth (Cm7-5), or a half-diminshed chord(Cφ7). Both of these names mean the same chord and is sort of a "you say po-tah-to, I say po-tay-to" situation. As long as you know this, you will be okay reading lead sheets! I have found that most people can encode the Cm7-5 symbol with greater ease, so I tend to use it. Either one is correct. Here are examples:

4

The sound of this chord is intense and was favored by composers like Richard Wagner and Richard Strauss eons before Jazz music was even an inkling in anyone's mind. Jazz musicians like Charlie Parker and Dizzy Gillespie adopted this chord in their be-bop compositions to raise their music to another level beyond just playing dance music. The minor-seventh with the flatted fifth became an integral part of the harmonic landscape of Jazz as it evolved through the late forties and early fifties. There is a music school in Los Angeles called "The School of the Flatted Fifth".

The last chord in the five basic chords is the full diminished chord which contains a root, a minor third, and flatted fifth, and a double- flatted seventh. It can also be represented by two symbols: C dim. 7 or C°7. Either symbol is correct.

Here is an example of how the chord would look on paper:

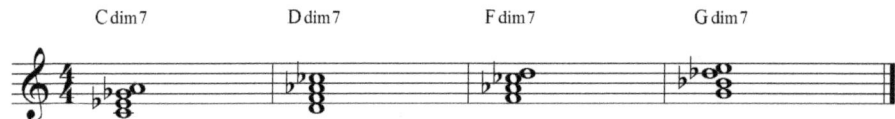

The diminished chord is unique in that it belongs to no diatonic key structure. Its' internal structure is also unparalleled by any other chord in that it is composed of all minor thirds. All other chords have varieagated intervals in their make-up. The sound of the diminished chord was described as "nebulous" by Claude Debussy.

It is often used as a bridge between two diatonic chords, such as a I chord (Major 7th) going to a II chord (minor seventh). So the progression would Read: I-#I-dim.-II-#IIdim., etc.

If the diminished chord were a part of speech, it would probably be a conjunction! Fats Waller was a composer who loved diminished chords. If we look at the chord progression for his tune "Aint Misbehavin'", we see a series of diatonic chords artfully interspersed with diminished seventh chords. This makes the song much more interesting and pulls it along with a sense of urgency!

Aint Misbehavin'

Fats Waller

This completes the discussion of the five basic seventh chords. At a later point, we can go into more complex chord structures such as 9ths, 11ths, and 13ths. It is advisable to become very adept at using the basic seventh and sixth chords before going on to higher degree chords.

Study the following sheets with seventh chords diligently and try to memorize each of the chords so that they can be automatically recalled when reading a "lead sheet". You must know at a glance what category each of the chords belongs in (Major, dominant, minor, half-diminished, and diminished), and be able to play the chord without thinking. This requires lots of repetition. It is a good idea to review the Major scales before playing the chords in each key. You should be able to play the chords in both hands, although initially you will be playing them in the left hand, as the right hand will be playing the melody. You might make some flash-cards from 3x5 inch index cards to quiz yourself daily on your increasing chord acumen. Learn them well in "root position" (root of the chord on the bottom), as later we will be playing the chords in their inverted forms.

Knowing your chords is the first step to becoming a Jazz pianist! I hope you will find this study fun and empowering.

Seventh Chord Vocabulary

29
F♯Maj7 F♯7 F♯m7 F♯m7-5 F♯dim7 C♯Maj7 C♯7
36
C♯m7 C♯m7-5 C♯dim7 F Maj7 F 7 F m7 F m7-5 F dim7
44
B♭Maj7 B♭7 B♭m7 B♭m7-5 B♭dim7 E♭Maj7 E♭7
51
E♭m7 E♭m7-5 E♭dim7 A♭Maj7 A♭7 A♭m7 A♭m7-5
58
A♭dim7 D♭Maj7 D♭7 D♭m7 D♭m7-5 D♭dim7 G♭Maj7

Memorize these chords so that you can respond to the symbol instantly. Chords should be practiced in both hands, either alternately or together. It is always a good idea to play the Major scale associated with each set of seventh chords. Practice sight-reading a new "lead sheet" out of a fake book every day after you go over the chords.

Your Notes

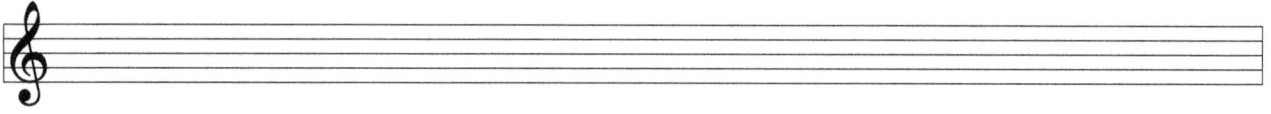

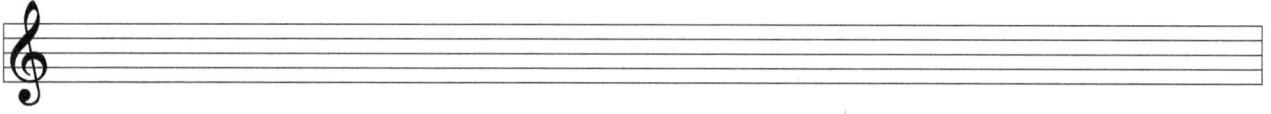

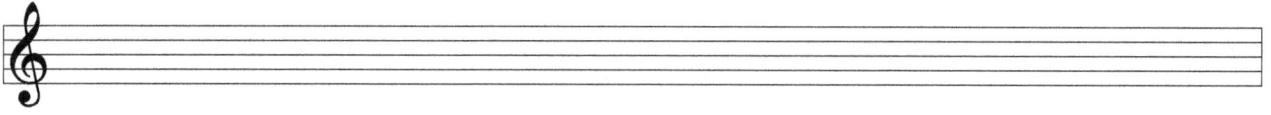

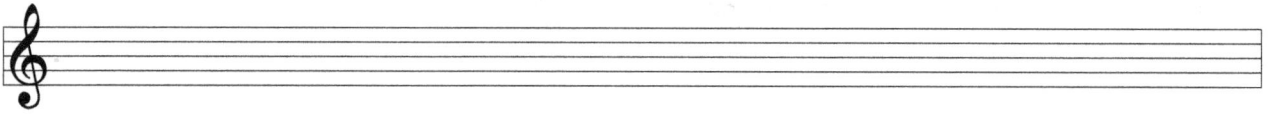

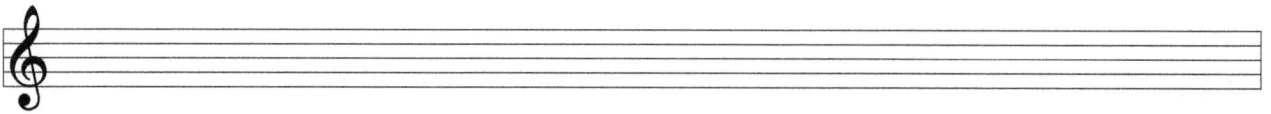

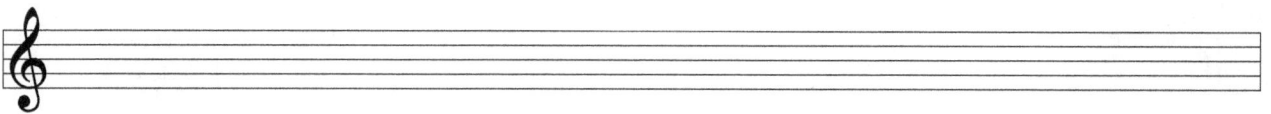

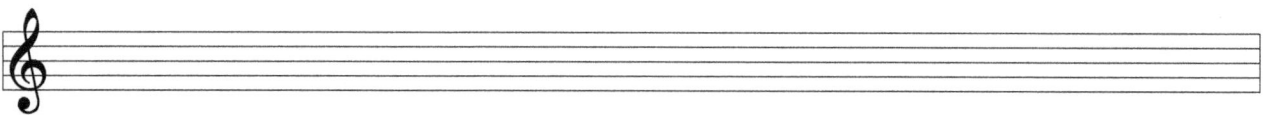

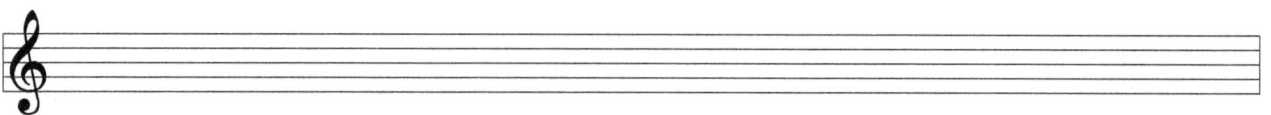

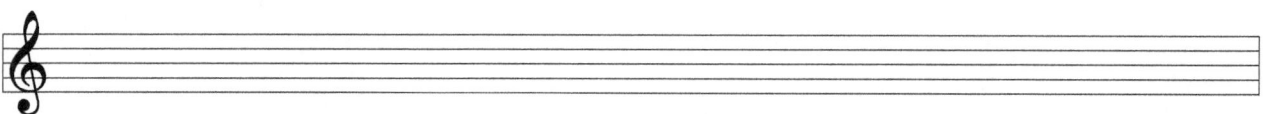

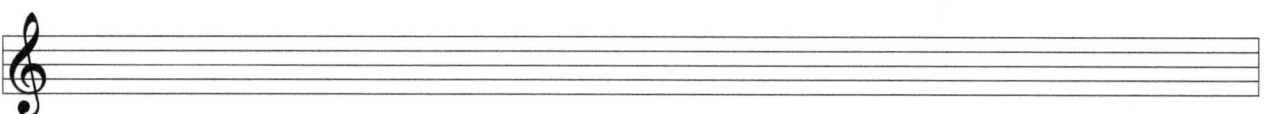

How to Read a "Lead Sheet"

The first way you will use Jazz chords in a song is in what we call "closed position voicing". We use the whole chord or an inversion of the chord in the left hand to accompany the right hand which plays the melody. We read the melody from a "lead sheet". Lead sheets give us two pieces of Information: the *melody* and the *chord symbols*. Lead sheets are written in the treble clef. Jazz pianists do not need the bass clef as they are generally making up their own arrangements.

Here is "Mack the Knife" with some sample chords added to the bass clef; You can continue adding chords yourself as you build your chord recognition skills. You may notice in this song that "G7" chords become "G9" chords. In this voicing, the G9 contains the fifth, the seventh, the ninth, and the third (from the bottom up), enabling a smoother transition from the Dm7 chord. Why? By using the G9 we are able to keep three "common tones" from the Dm7 chord. To move to the G9 we only have to drop the seventh tone of the Dm7 chord down one-half step to the B, and, voila, we have a G9 chord. The rule is: the more common tones we can keep, the smoother the transition.

Mack the Knife

Kurt Weill

Mack the Knife #2

Your Notes

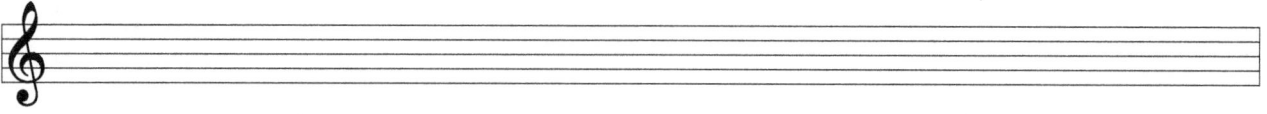

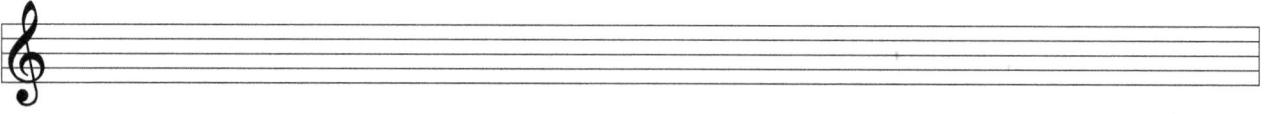

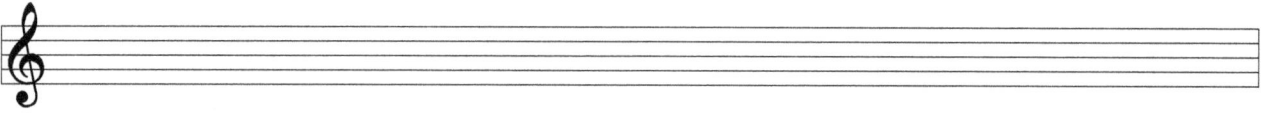

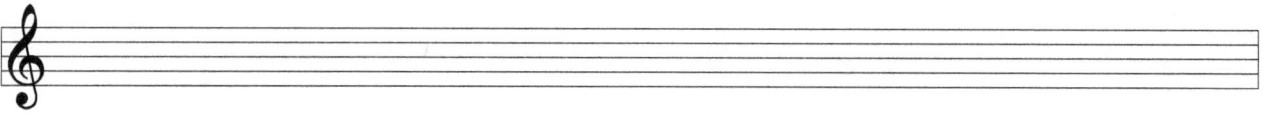

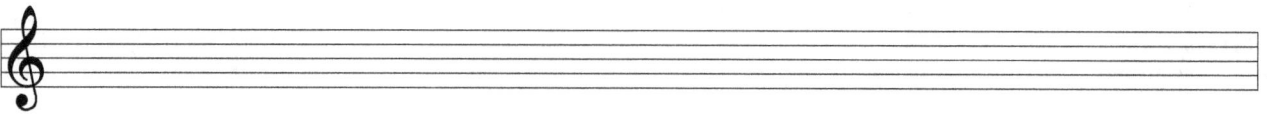

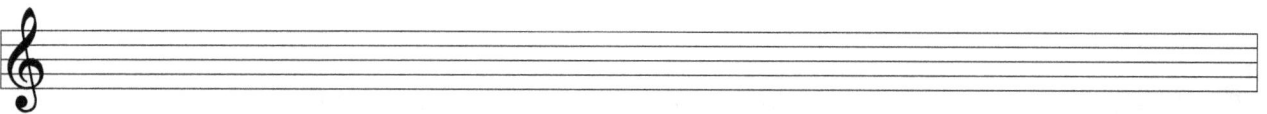

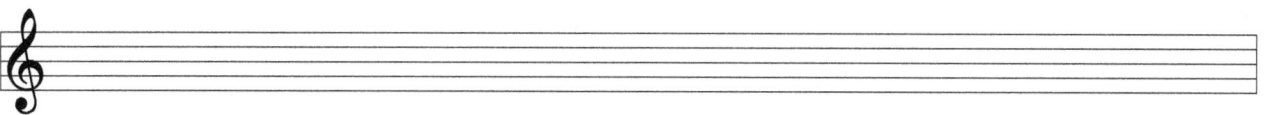

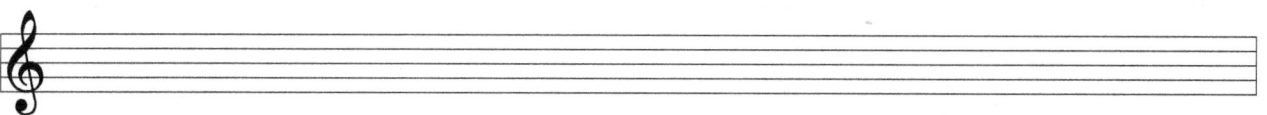

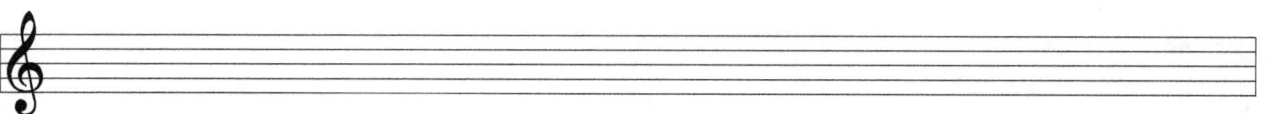

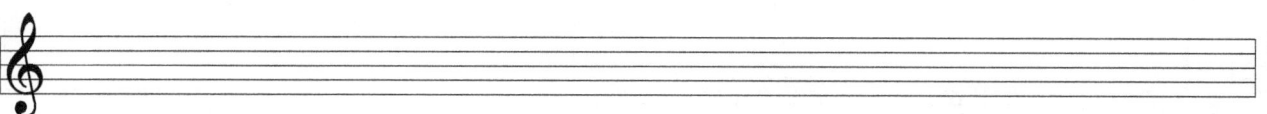

Diatonic Chords: How the Chords Interact with Each Other

Now that you have learned some of the seventh chords in various keys, it is time to see how they might interact with each other in a real song. The word "diatonic" comes from the Greek language and translates as "up the staircase". So diatonic chords are the chords that are built on each one of the seven scale tones.

The diatonic chords in each key are of different types, and work together to form a "musical syntax" much like words that are different parts of speech work together to form sentences. Each Major scale has two Major seventh chords built on the first and fourth degrees:

The Major sevenths have a pretty, stable sound and if they were words in a sentence they probably would function as nouns.

Each key also contains three minor sevenths built on the second, third, and sixth degrees (II, III, and VI). They work in tandem with the Major sevenths and the dominant seventh. They have a passive sound and if they were a part of speech they might function as an adverb.

There is only one dominant seventh chord in each key and it is always built on the fifth tone of the Major scale. The dominant chord has a very vibrant, active sound. What part of speech would this chord be? If you guessed "verb" you would be right!

The last chord we will look at is the one built on the seventh tone of the scale which is called the half-diminshed. It is also called The minor-seventh with a flatted fifth. If this chord were a part of speech, it might function as a conjunction.

Here are examples of how this chord might appear:

What do we do with all this information about diatonic chords? The first thing would be to go through all your scales and try writing the diatonic chords on each of the scale tones:

The next thing would be to separate the chords in genres:

Practice these chords in groups in each key: Major, minor, dominant, and half-diminished. You will be on your way to understanding how music works: in other words, predictable ways in which chords want to move. In Jazz music, we call these predictable movements "progressions". We will start by looking at the most basic movement in Jazz harmony, the II-V-I progression.

Chapter II: The II-V-I Progression: the DNA of Jazz

One of the most basic ways that Western harmony moves (besides diatonically) is in root movement by fourths. Here is an example in the key of C:

This movement in fourths is as predictable as the evening tide, and has been used by great composers from Beethoven to Charlie Parker. The next chapter will go into further detail on how a Jazz pianist might "voice" the chords in the left hand.

The II-V-I progression is probably the DNA of Jazz; The II and V chords work together symbiotically to move musical phrases toward their ultimate destination of resolution.

Why II-V? These two chords move in the interval of a perfect fourth toward the I or tonic chord. This motion is one of the basic ways Western harmony moves. Some other ways are: diatonically (up the scale), and chromatically (in half-steps). Root movement by fourths is the fundamental way Western harmony moves. Some musicologists trace it back to ancient China where archeologists found stone drums that were all tuned in fourths and fifths! Neurolinguists have a theory that the human brain is "hard-wired" for music in fourths or fifths much like babies all over the world say some form of the word "Mama".

Here are some examples of the II-V progression:

Of course it would be extremely awkward for a pianist's left hand to be jumping in fourths all the time. Usually Jazz pianists can easily move from the II chord to the V by simply dropping the "7th" of the II chord down one half-step. The ensuing new chord then becomes a rootless V chord (or V9), which works especially well when playing with a bassist, as he would normally be playing the root. Even when playing solo piano, the V9 chord sounds better than the V7.

Satin Doll excerpt

Duke Ellington

It is quite easy to recognize the II-V "pairs" in a song. The II chord is always a minor seventh, and the V chord is always a dominant seventh. The V chord is always a perfect fourth higher than the II chord. A Jazz pianist begins the study of a song by mentally scanning for the II-V "pairs"; at first, you can use a blue pencil to draw arrows between the II and the V chord:

Dm7 → G7

A good idea is to pencil in the Roman numeral number of the chord above the letter symbol. This way you always see how the progression moves. You can then "encode" the song in Roman numerals on an index card and try to play it using just the outline of the progression. You will then easily memorize the melody and not have to rely on reading it every time.

The next step would be to try the song in several different keys. This is where the REAL MUSICAL GROWTH OCCURS.

Let's now look at the II-V progression in all the keys. You will notice that when we get to the Gm7-C9 II-V, it is spelled in two versions, the root position and the inverted position. The reason for this is that at this point on the keyboard, the chords are getting a bit too high in range, both for the sound and possible interference with the right hand's activity. The ideal range for closed position Jazz chords is between E below Middle C to G above Middle C.

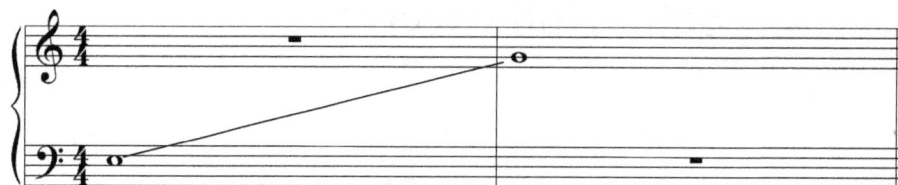

This is the ideal range for closed position Jazz chords! Here is the Dm7-G9 II-V. Jazz musicians think in "numbers" So that they know exactly what they are playing:

This is the Gm7-C9 II-V in root position:

This is the Gm7-C9 II-V in it's "pivot" position with the seventh tone of the Gm7 chord now on the bottom:

You are now ready to proceed to the next page of the II-V's in all keys! Commit them to memory muscularly and mentally!

II-V drop 7 ex

BMaj7

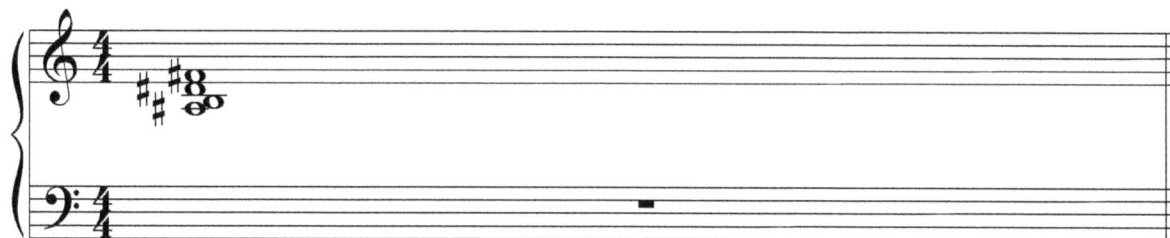

Practice the II-V-I progressions in your left hand until they are totally automatic for you. The mastery of the left-hand chords frees your right hand to concentrate on playing the melody with interesting phrasing. When you begin improvising, the left-hand chords must be at your command.

Your Notes

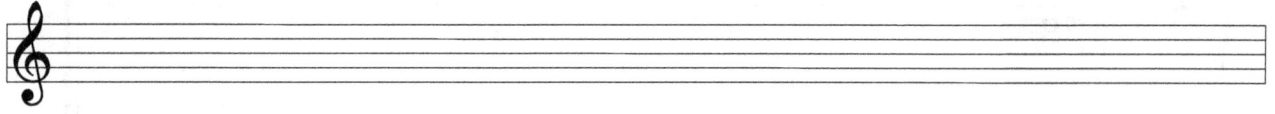

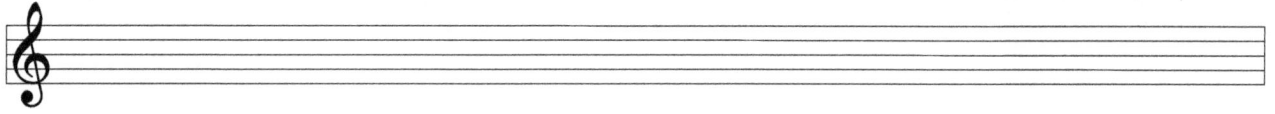

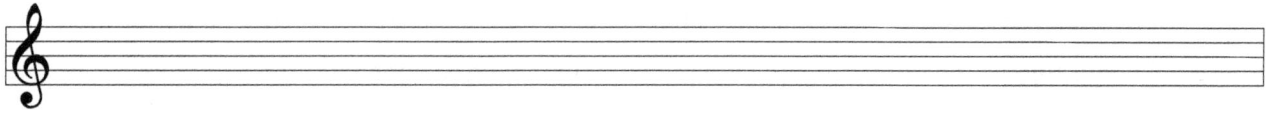

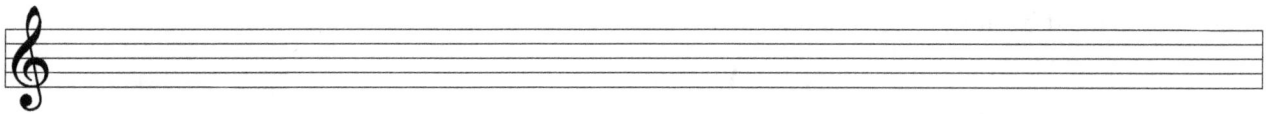

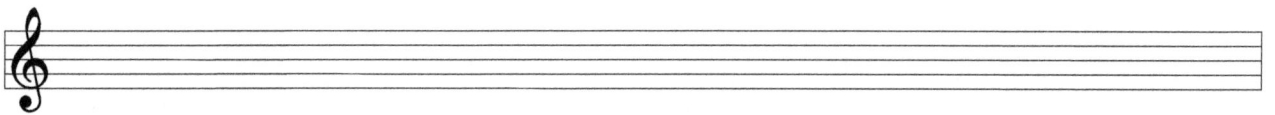

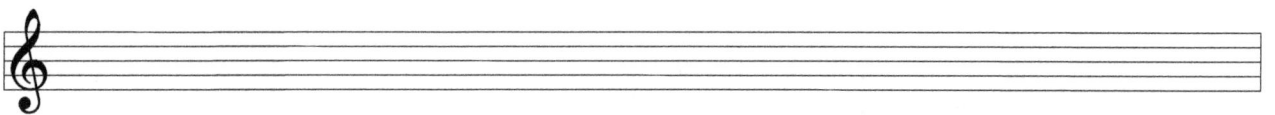

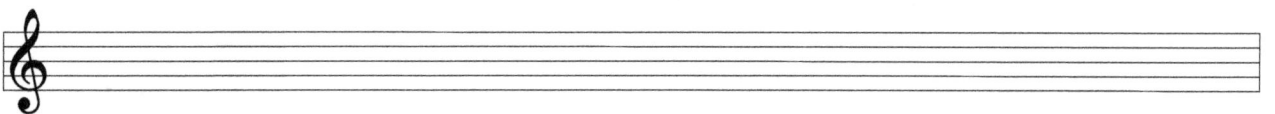

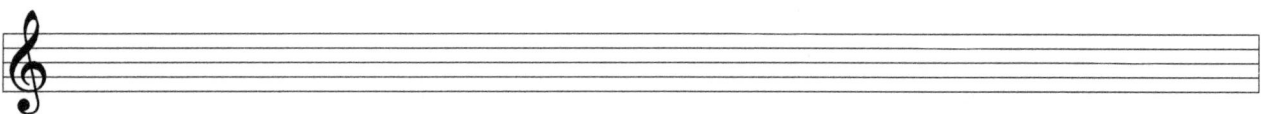

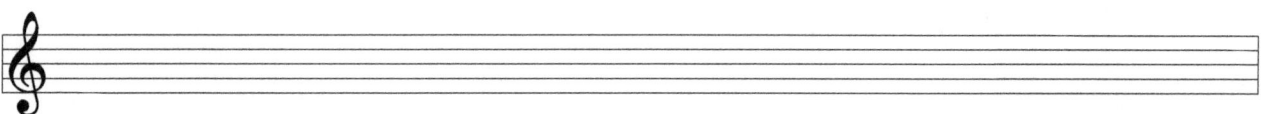

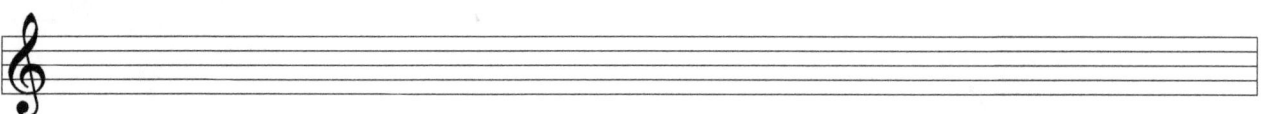

Satin Doll: An All American Classic Song

Duke Ellington wrote this song in 1953 in collaboration with Billy Strayhorn who wrote some sentimental lyrics. Johnny Mercer was hired later to rewrite the lyrics in a more commercial style, and the song became a hit. Duke often Used "Satin Doll" as an opening and closing song for his concerts, and pianists today still consider it one of the top ten requested songs. Harmonically, it is a perfectly crafted mosaic of II-V chords, and is considered an unusual progression as it starts on a II-V, not a I chord. you will see that the first phrase has a lot of momentum and does not come in for a "landing" until the first ending.

Satin Doll

Duke Ellington
Arr.:L. Hoffman

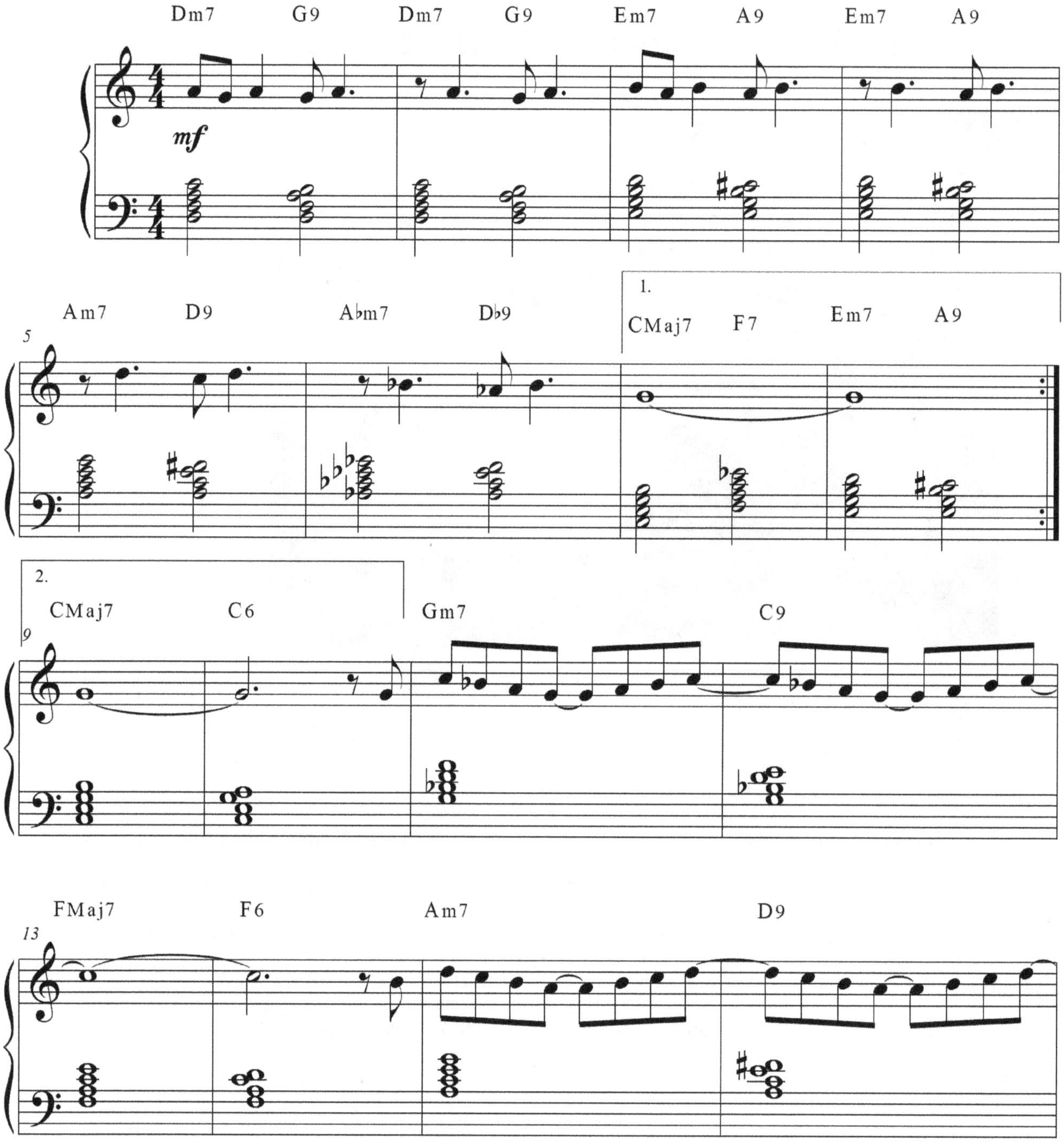

Dm7 G9 Dm7 G9 Dm7 G9
17
switch-e - roo - nee
Em7 A9 Em7 A9 Am7 D9 Abm7 Db9
21
C7 B7 Bb7 A7 Am7 D9 Abm7 Db9
25
C13#11
29

When the Saints Go Marching In

James Black

When the Saints Go Marching In #2

James Black

Harold Arlen: An American Songwriter

Harold Arlen was one of the most prolific songwriters of the Twentieth Century. He moved to New York City at a young age to pursue his career as a performing pianist and composer. He was later hired by Metro Goldwyn Mayer to create film scores, and began collaborating with the lyricist "Yip" Harburg. In 1938 they wrote the music for the film "The Wizard of Oz", and their ballad from the score "Over the Rainbow" became the best song of the year. It was also recorded by the Glenn Miller Orchestra the same year and it was #2 on the Hit Parade. Harold Arlen knew he had to write an epic ballad for "Wizard", but was experiencing writer's block. He took his wife Anya out for an ice cream soda one afternoon, and when they came out of Schawb's Drug Store, they saw a beautiful rainbow. Harold went right home to pen "Over the Rainbow", which has become an American classic. Mr. Arlen was also noted for creating a "bluesy" element in his songs. Some of the songs that exemplified this trend were: "Blues in the Night", "Stormy Weather", and "Black Coffee".

Over the Rainbow

H.Arlen
arr.:L. Hoffman

Chapter III: Voicing the Chords

Open Position Chords

Now that you have played "Over the Rainbow" in closed position, let's try it in open position. In this way of voicing the chords, the sound becomes more opaque and sophisticated. The left hand plays only the root and the seventh of the chords, and is commonly called a "shell". The right hand plays the melody note and, below the melody, adds the third and sometimes doubles the seventh when possible. Here is how the first phrase of the song would look:

You may notice that the root and bass notes are the "outer voices" of the chord. In open position, there should be no note played above the melody note. The right hand plays the melody note (usually with the little finger), and also plays the 3rd of the chord underneath it:

The left hand plays the root and the seventh of the chord creating what Jazz pianists call a shell:

Together, both hands play all the elements of the chord making a beautiful translucent sound.

This treatment of chords is called "voicing". Music arrangers do this all the time when writing "scores" for big bands and orchestras. You can do it at the piano today! By voicing chords, you are taking the first step towards writing for instrumental ensembles In the future.

Over the Rainbow:Open Position

H.Arlen

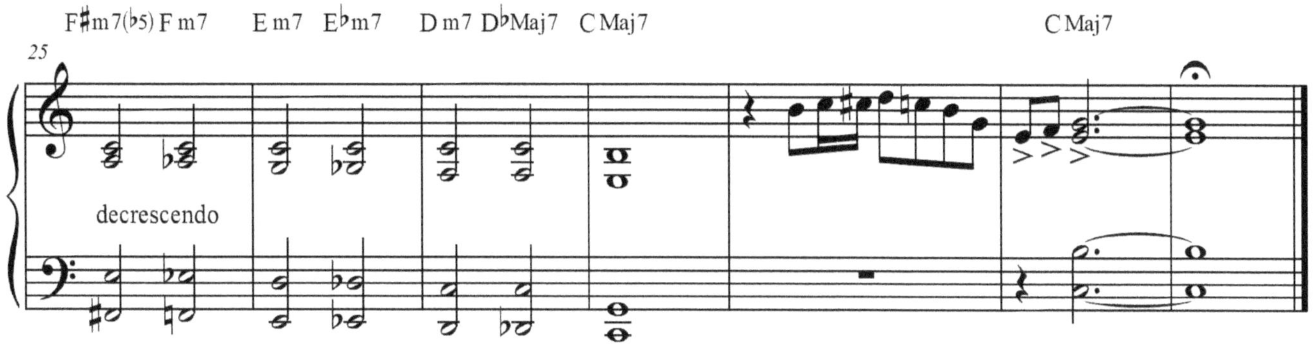

Your Notes

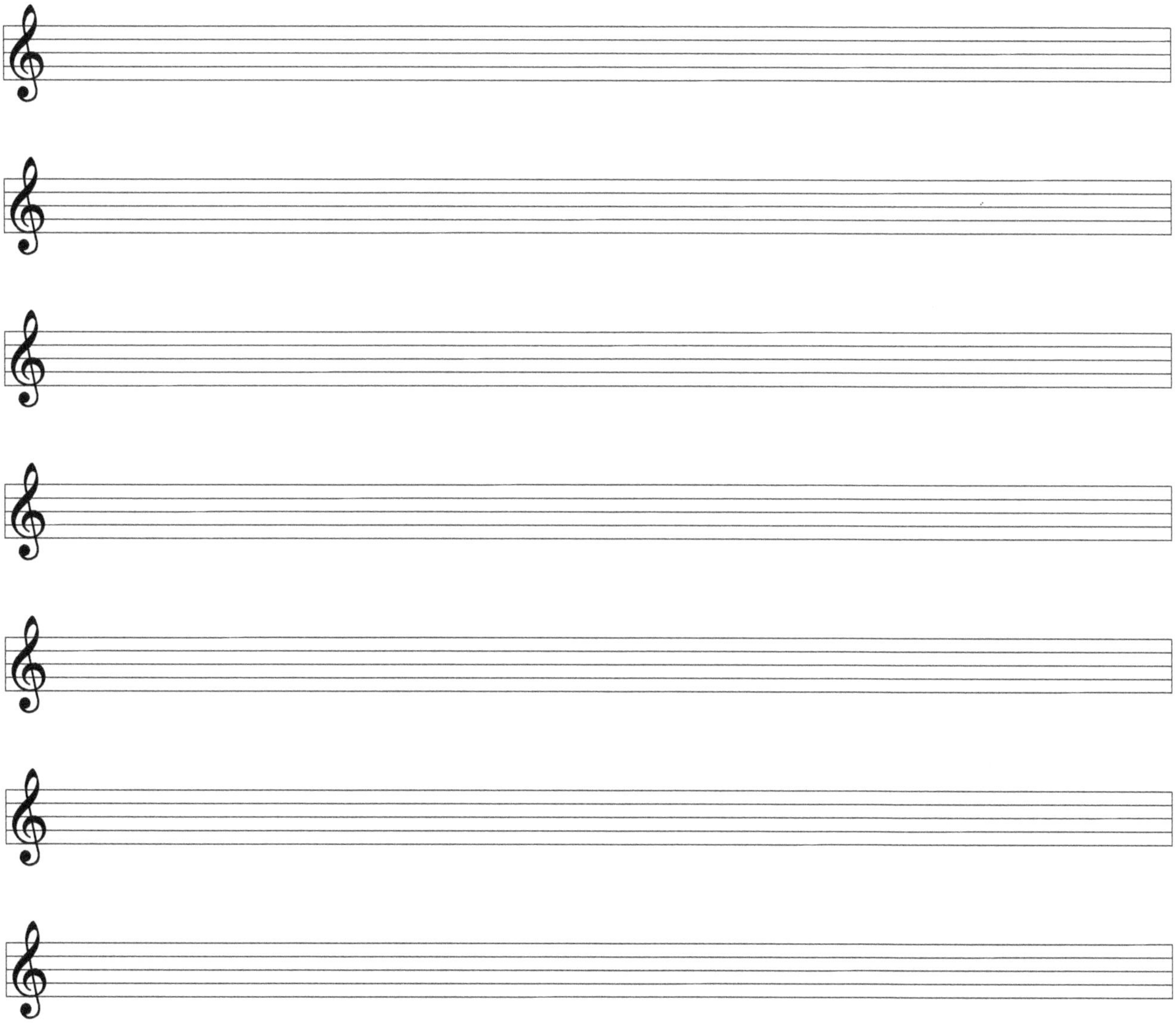

Over the Rainbow: a Hybrid Arrangement

H. Arlen

Sometimes you can combine different chord voicings in a single song. "Over the Rainbow's" melody dips into the lower register of the treble clef, forcing the chords to "split" into open voicings. The left hand plays the root and the seventh (or "shell"), and the right hand plays the melody, the third, and doubles the seventh when possible. The variegated texture of this type of treatment makes the arrangement interesting to the listener.

Modes: Scales Within A Scale

You may have marveled at hearing Jazz musicians like George Shearing or Charlie Parker as they rolled out one fantastic improvisation after another. You may have thought that you would have to be born with that kind of talent. You will be happy to know that Jazz music is like a science and can be learned in a step-by-step approach. All Jazz players learn various vocabularies which they use to create those great solos! One of the most important things they learn is how to play modes. Each degree of the Major scale has it's own scale which is called a "mode". Each mode then corresponds with the diatonic chord which Is built on the scale tone.

There are seven modes:

The modes come from ancient Greece and are named for various regions of Greece. Jazz musicians rediscovered these modes and used them to create improvisations that blend with the chords of the song. Before Jazz came into it's present state of sophistication, musicians would play chord tones to create solos. Artists like Dizzy Gillespie and Charlie Parker gravitated towards modal improvisations as they strove to create elaborate solos that would intrigue listeners. Some of their solos were so good that they became songs in their own right. Take a look at the exercises on the next page and try the modes in various keys. You should "swing" the eighth notes so that they have a LONG-SHORT feel. This rhythm is the dialect of Jazz.

Jazz Modes

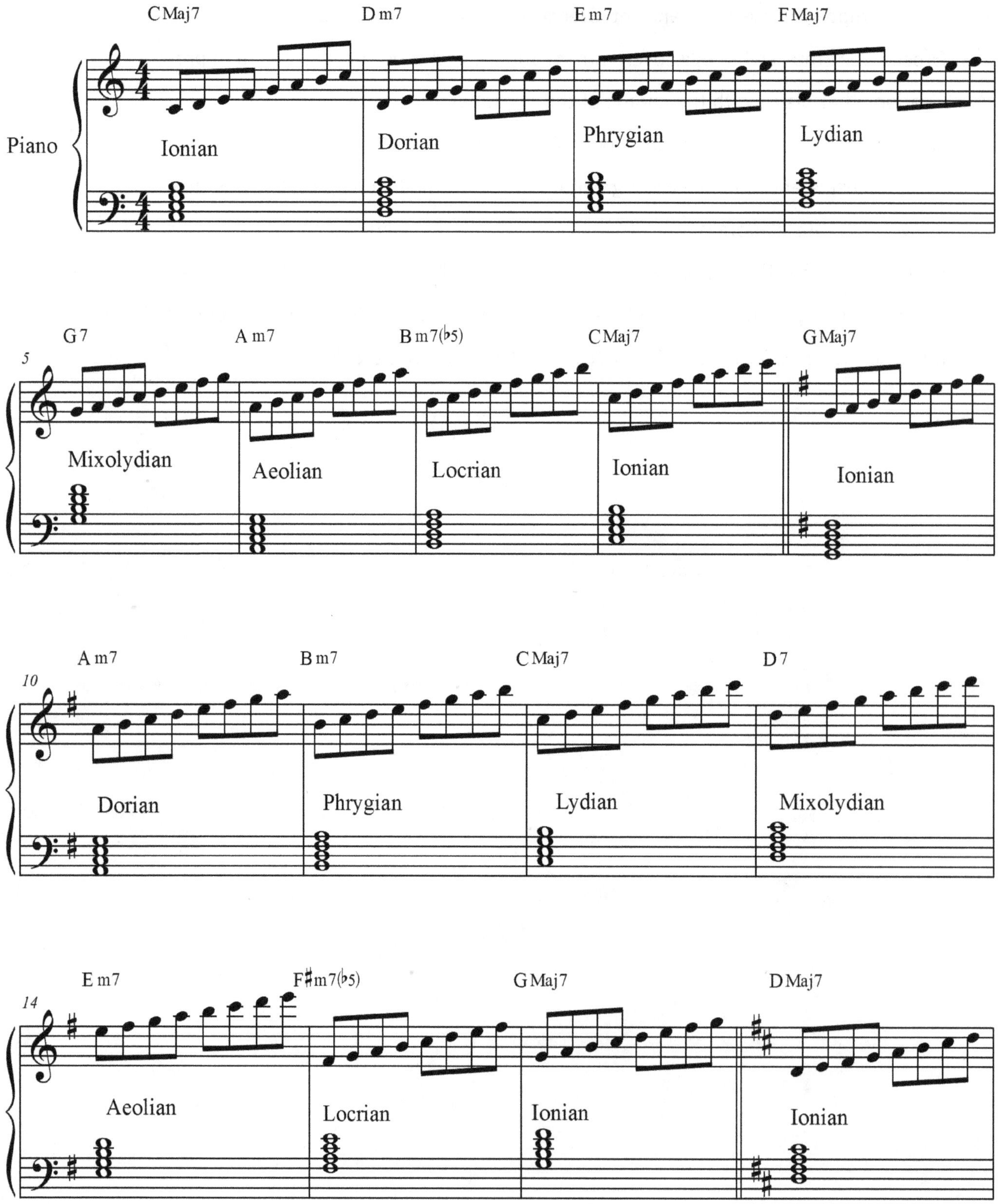
CMaj7
Dm7
Em7
FMaj7
Piano
Ionian
Dorian
Phrygian
Lydian
G7
Am7
Bm7(♭5)
CMaj7
GMaj7
Mixolydian
Aeolian
Locrian
Ionian
Ionian
Am7
Bm7
CMaj7
D7
Dorian
Phrygian
Lydian
Mixolydian
Em7
F♯m7(♭5)
GMaj7
DMaj7
Aeolian
Locrian
Ionian
Ionian

You can continue writing these modes in all the rest of the keys in your practice notebook. Choose several keys daily and play through each of the modes. You can then test yourself to see if you can automatically play a given mode in any key. For example, play the dorian mode in the key of G, mixolydian mode in the key of A, and Phrygian mode in the key of F. This type of practice will enable you to play "spontaneously" after you play the melody of any song. Remember, the second chorus should be your own improvisation. Complete command of the modes leads to your own creations!

Using Modes In A Song: "Dearly Beloved"

"Dearly Beloved" was written by Jerome Kern and Johnny Mercer in 1942. The song was introduced by Fred Astaire when he sang it in the film "You Were Never Love-lier". Now that you are familiar with modes, "Dearly Beloved" Is an ideal harmonic landscape for you to use them in the context of an actual song. Learn the melody and chords first, And then try the variations which use the modes and patterns. The first eight bars of the song use only the Dm7-G7 chords, So you will get a chance to practice the Dorian mode in the Key of C!

Use these blank staffs to make any sketches of your own Ideas for improvisations:

Your Notes

Your Notes

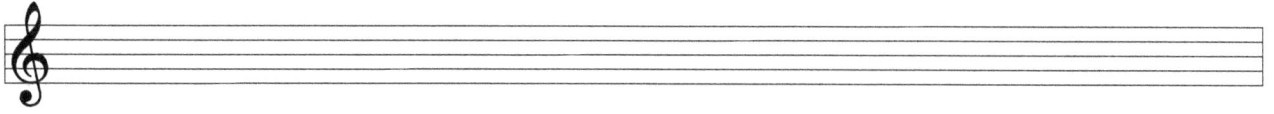

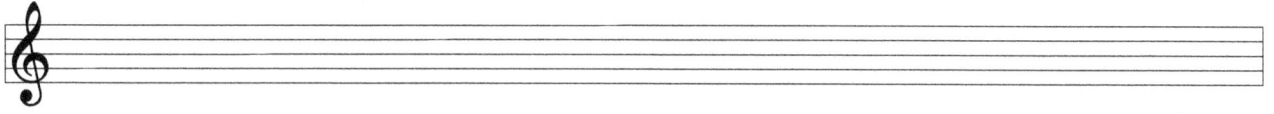

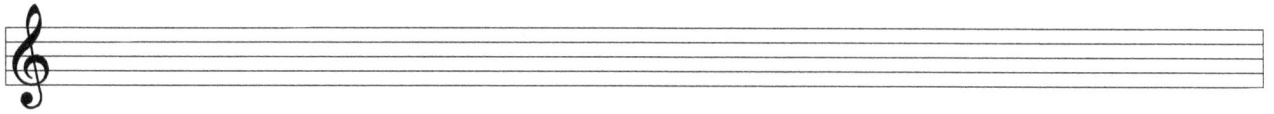

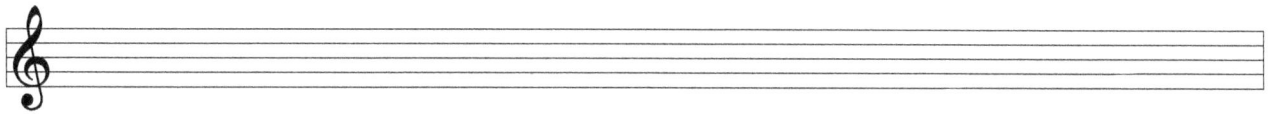

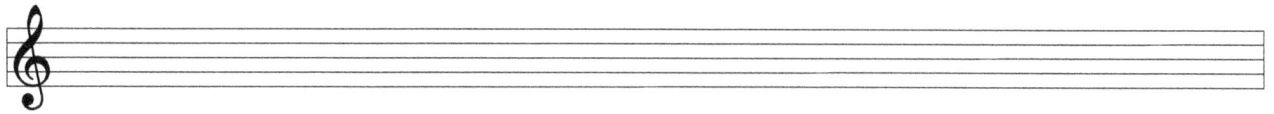

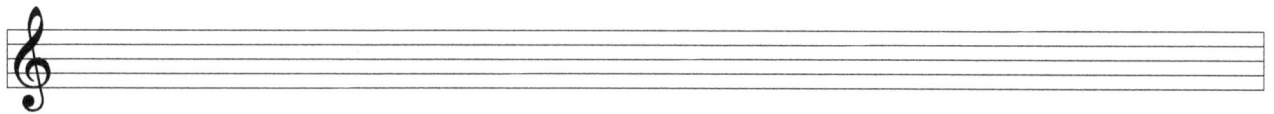

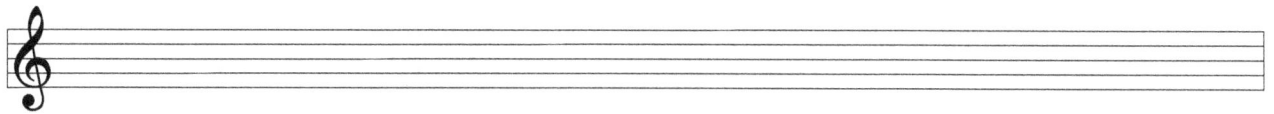

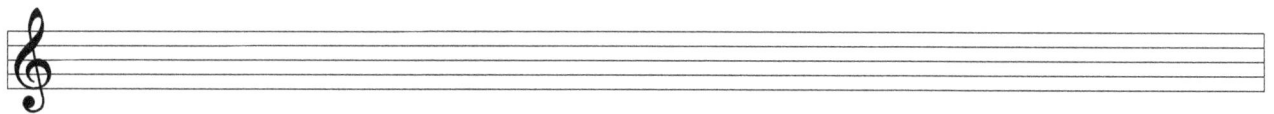

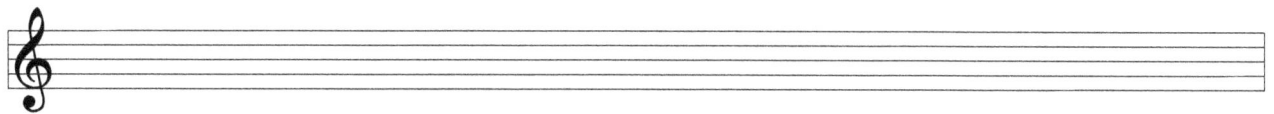

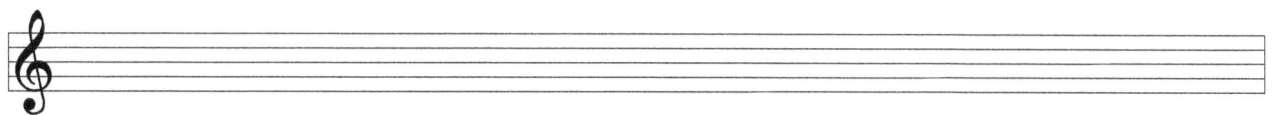

Your Notes

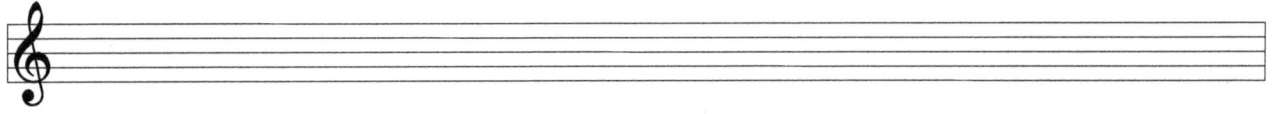

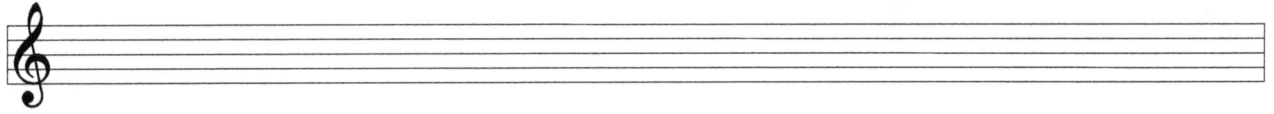

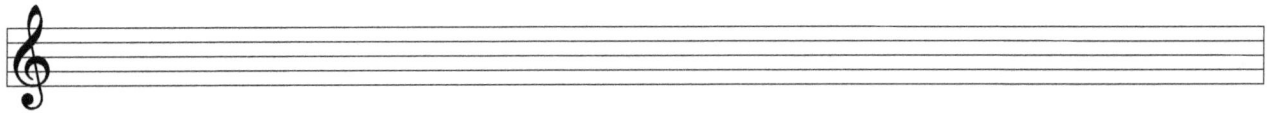

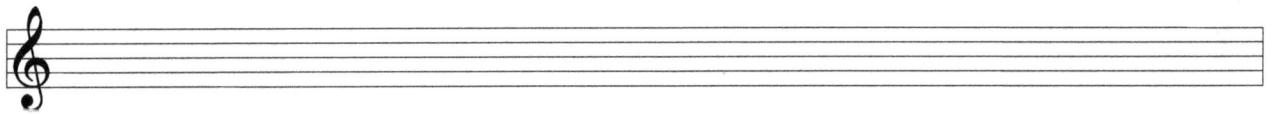

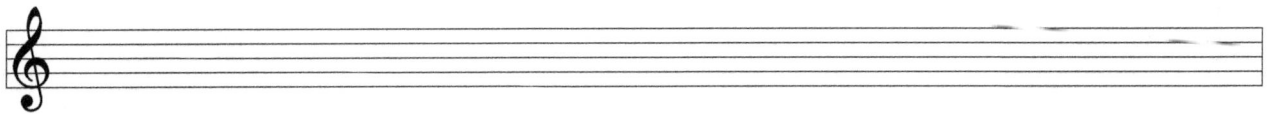

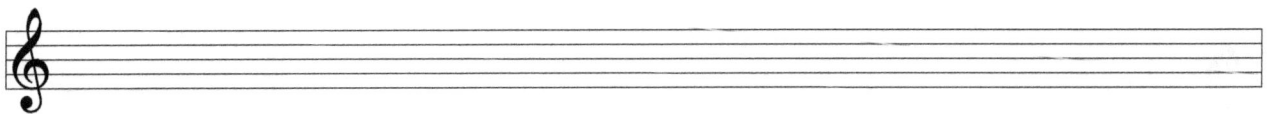

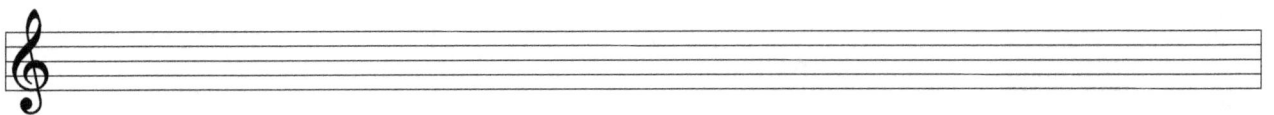

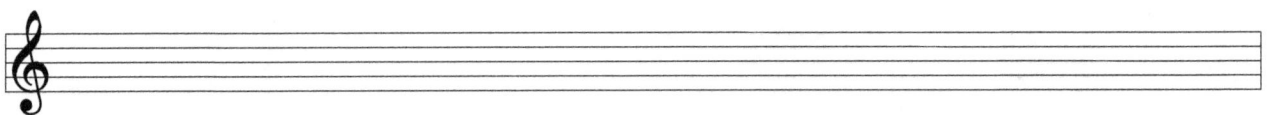

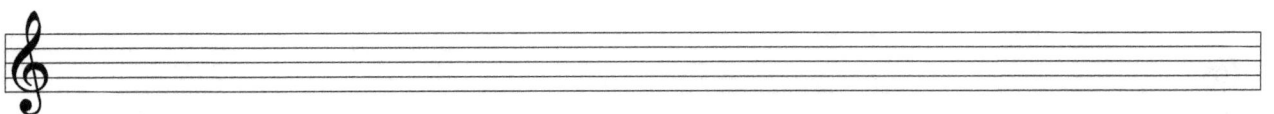

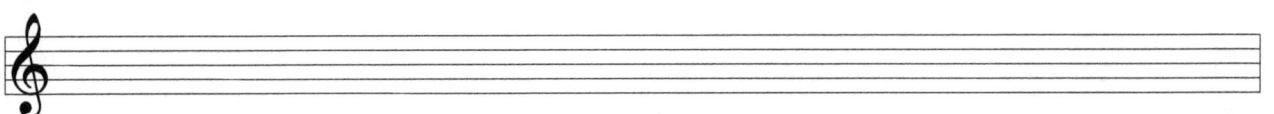

Dearly Beloved

Kern/arr. L. Hoffman

Go to Dearly Beloved #2

Dearly Beloved #2

Kern/arr. L. Hoffman

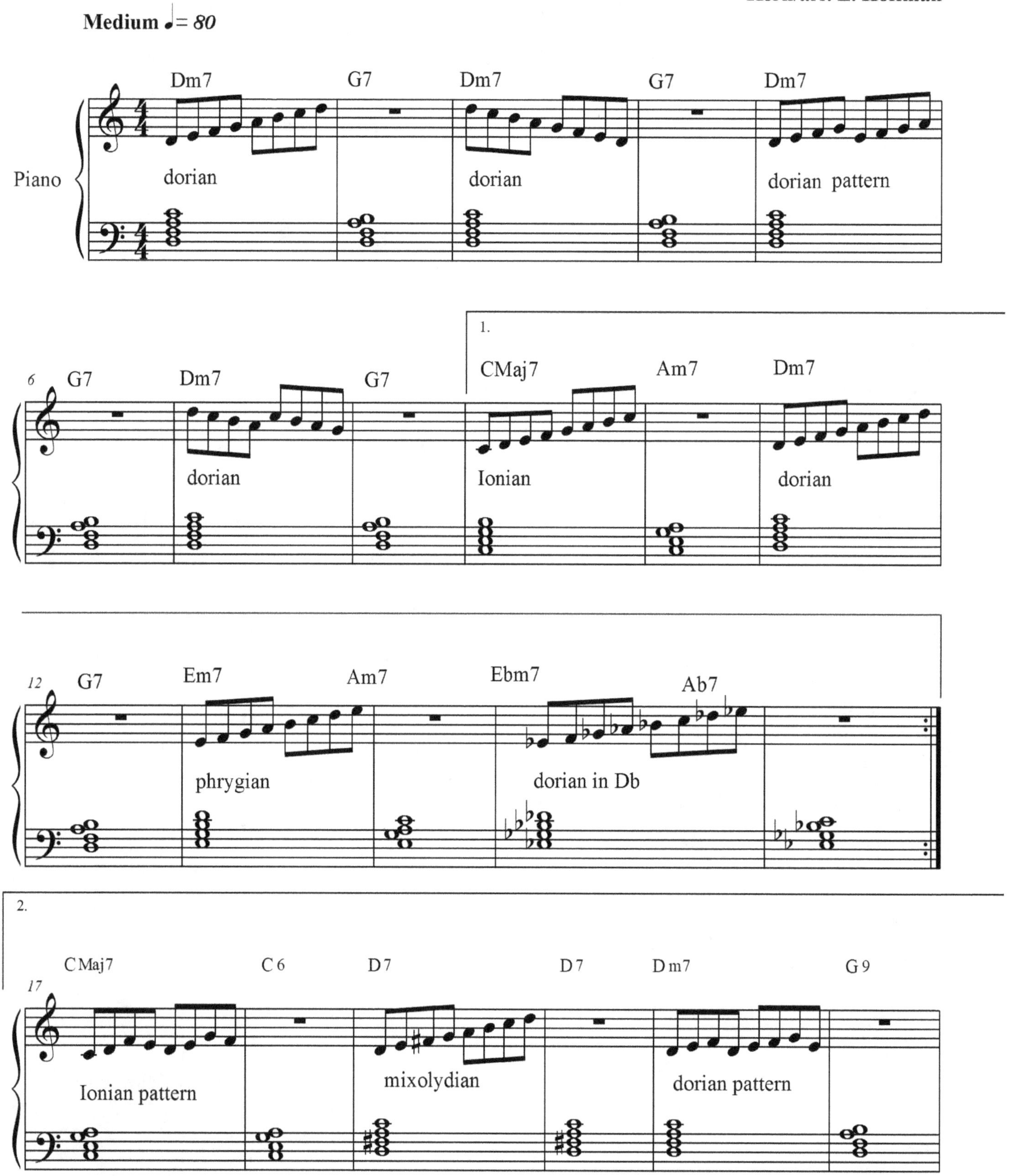

Dearly Beloved #2

Dearly Beloved #3 Rhythmic Displacement

Kern/arr. L. Hoffman

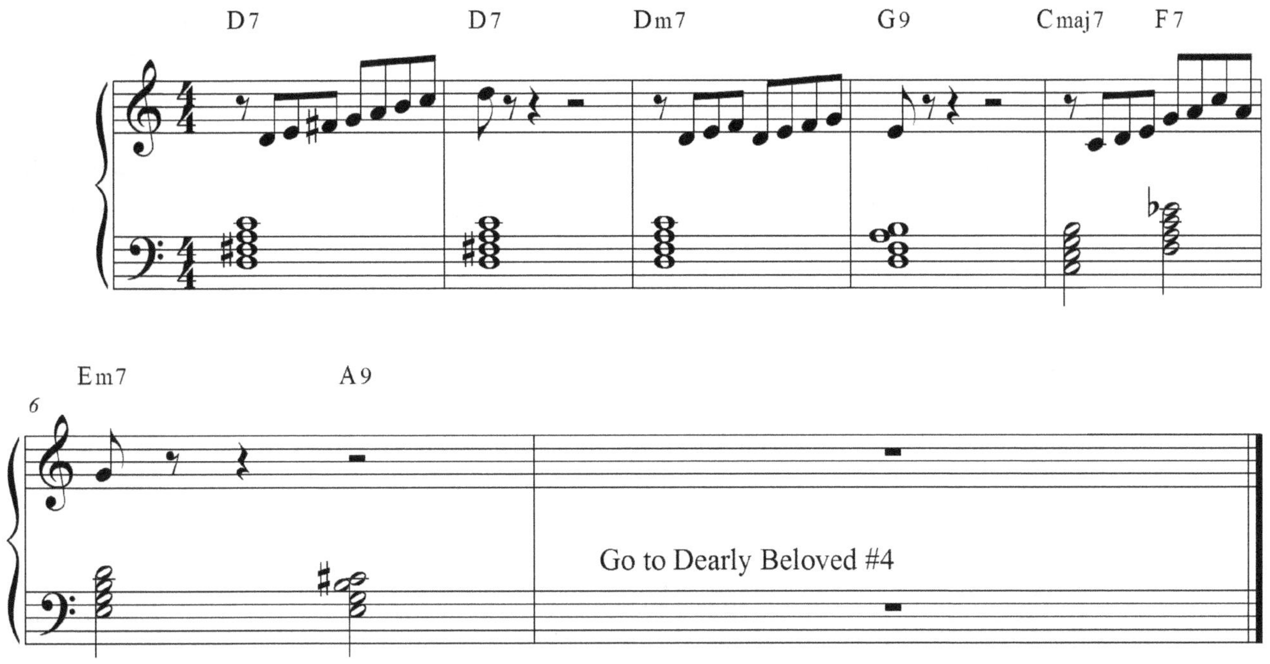
D7
D7
Dm7
G9
Cmaj7
F7
6
Em7
A9
Go to Dearly Beloved #4

Dearly Beloved #4 Dorian/Blues

Kern/arr. L. Hoffman

Dearly Beloved #4 Dorian/Blues

Dearly Beloved #5 Bluesy

Kern/arr. L, Hoffman

Dearly Beloved #5 Bluesy

In this version of "Dearly Beloved", the left hand plays four chords per measure with accents on the second and fourth beats, creating a "backbeat" effect. This rendition was inspired by the style of Erroll Garner who was famous for his rhythmic stylings.
The right hand freely improvises in a bluesy manner.

Dearly Beloved #6 Shapes

Kern/arr. L. Hottman

Dearly Beloved #6 Shapes

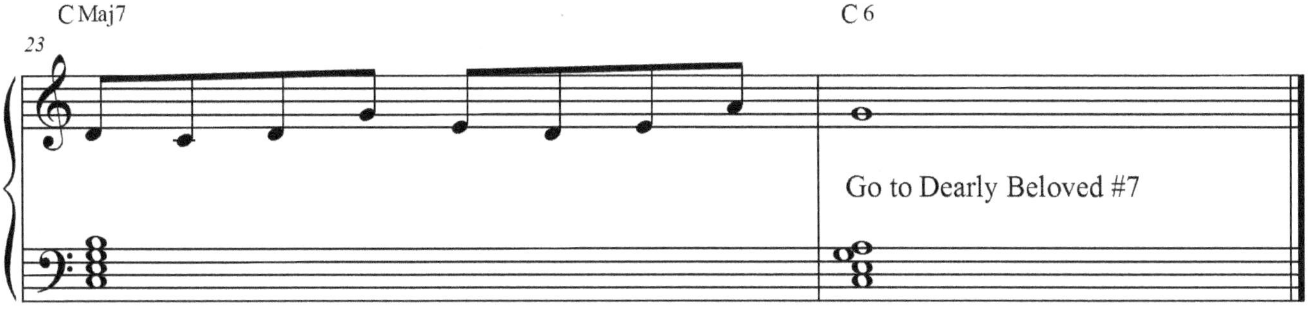
C Maj7
C 6
23
Go to Dearly Beloved #7

Dearly Beloved #7 Chord Variants

Kern/arr. L. Hoffman

Dearly Beloved #7 Chord Variants

Go to Var.#8

Dearly Beloved #8 Inertia

Kern/arr. L. Hoffman

Dearly Beloved #8 Inertia

I hope you have enjoyed reading and playing the musical examples in this book.
You are now ready to try creating your own arrangements! You can purchase
one of the many "fake books" on the market and use the chord knowledge you
now have to play your unique version of Standard tunes! Happy playing!

Your Notes

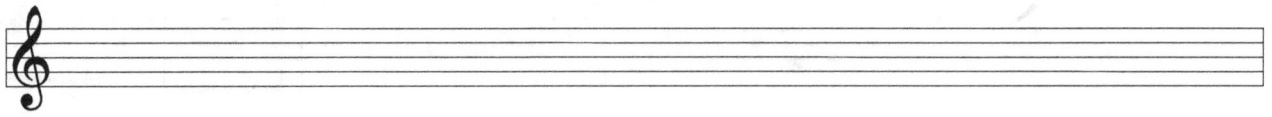
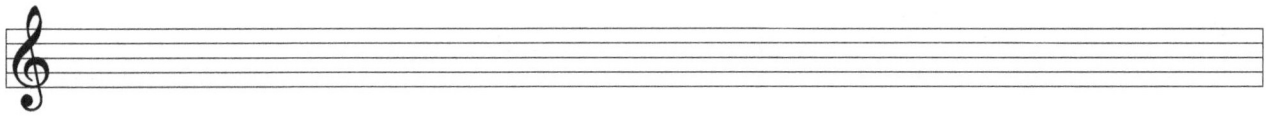
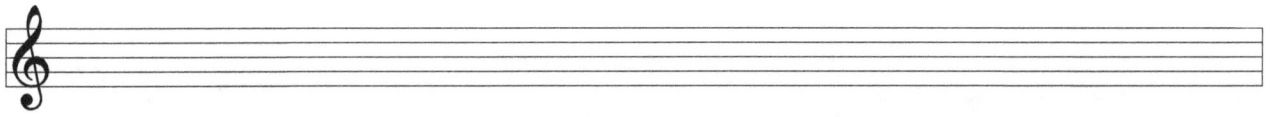
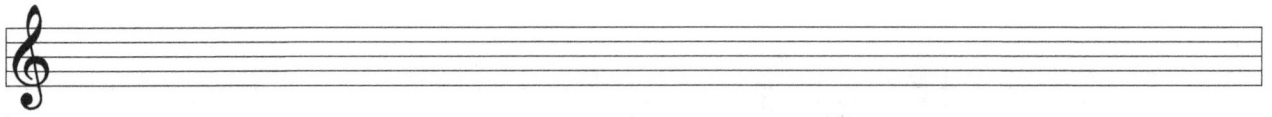
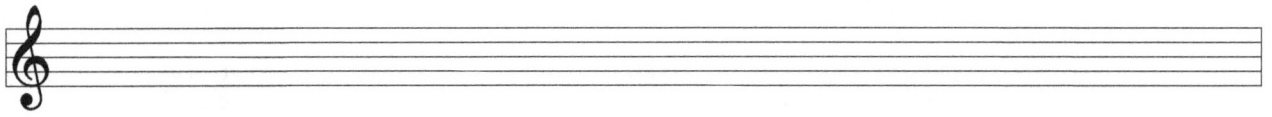
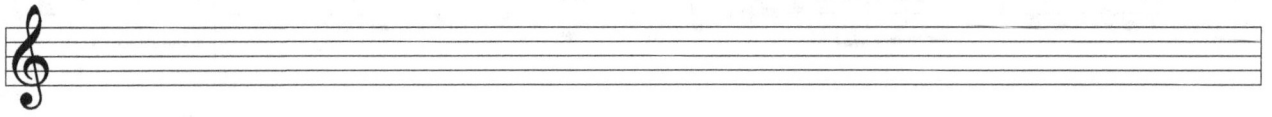
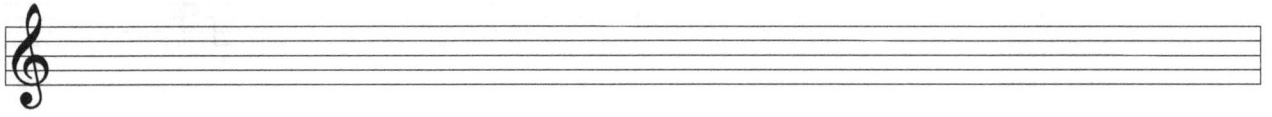
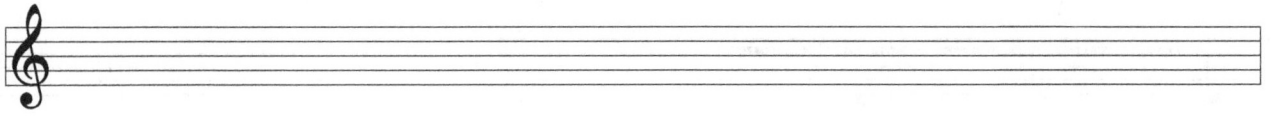
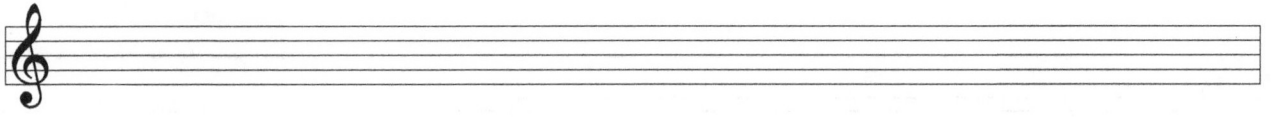
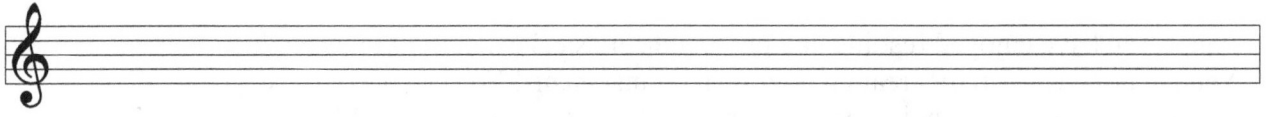